LET'S CELEBRATE

Martin Luther King, Jr.

and His Birthday

by Jacqueline Woodson
pictures by Floyd Cooper

Silver Press

Produced by Kirchoff/Wohlberg, Inc.
Text copyright © 1990 Kirchoff/Wohlberg, Inc.
Illustrations copyright © 1990 Floyd Cooper and
Kirchoff/Wohlberg, Inc.

Published by Silver Press, a division of Silver Burdett Press, Inc.
Simon & Schuster, Inc., Prentice Hall Bldg., Englewood Cliffs, NJ 07632

Printed in the United States of America

10 9 8 7 6 5 4 3 2 1

Library of Congress Cataloging-in-Publication Data
Woodson, Jacqueline
Martin Luther King, Jr., and his birthday / by Jacqueline Woodson;
pictures by Floyd Cooper.
p. cm.—(Let's celebrate)
Summary: Describes the life of the civil rights worker who is
honored on Martin Luther King Day.
1. King, Martin Luther, Jr., 1929-1968—Juvenile literature.
2. Afro-Americans—Biography—Juvenile literature. 3. Baptists—
United States—Clergy—Biography—Juvenile literature. 4. Civil
rights workers—United States—Biography—Juvenile literature.
5. Martin Luther King Day—Juvenile literature. [1. King, Martin
Luther. Jr., 1929-1968. 2. Clergy. 3. Civil rights workers.
4. Afro-Americans—Biography. 5. Martin Luther King Day.]
I. Cooper, Floyd, ill. II. Title. III. Series.
E185.97.K5W66 1990
323′ .092—dc20   89-49536
[B]   CIP
[92]   AC
ISBN 0-671-69112-0   ISBN 0-671-69106-6 (lib. bdg.)

Martin Luther King, Jr.

and His Birthday

Young Martin Learns a Lesson

Martin ran down the block. He ran around the corner. It was his first day of school. He couldn't wait to tell his best friends about it.

Martin had been sad when he found out they would be going to different schools. But it almost didn't matter. Today had been so much fun.

Martin ran up to the door of his friends' house. "Go home, Martin," their mother said.

"Can't Tom and Billy come out to play?" Martin asked.

"I don't want my sons playing with colored children anymore."

Martin was surprised. Her voice sounded angry.

"But we've always played together," Martin said. He felt tears come into his eyes.

"Well, not anymore. It's time you learned. White kids and colored kids can't play together," she said. "Now go home."

Martin turned quickly. He didn't want her to see that he was crying. He couldn't believe it. He would never play with Billy and Tom again.

"Mama! Mama!" Martin cried. "Billy and Tom's mother said I can't play with them anymore! Why not, Mama?"

Martin's mother sat him on her lap. She brushed the tears out of his eyes.

"Some white people think we should be treated differently from them," she answered. "They think they are better than we are because our skin is brown and theirs is white."

"Is that why we have to go to different schools?" Martin asked.

His mother nodded. "Everything is divided in the South, Martin. Some things are for white people. Other things are for colored people," she said softly.

"When we go to the movies, we can't even
go through the same door as the white people, Mama.
It's not fair."

"You're right, Martin. It isn't fair. But it's the law.
We have to use different rest rooms. We can't drink out
of the same water fountains either," Martin's mother
reminded him.

"Are my white friends really better than I am,
Mama?"

"Of course not, Martin. You're as good as anybody."

The next Sunday, Martin followed behind his
brother and sister. They were on their way to church.
Their father was preaching.

"Sit still, Martin," his mother whispered. But it was hard for Martin to sit still. He was thinking about his best friends. He was thinking about the separate water fountains and schools and bathrooms.

"I want things to be different," Martin thought. "I want white people to stop thinking they're better than black people."

Martin looked around the church. The members were listening to his father preach. Martin knew he should be listening, too. But he wanted to swing his feet. He wanted to turn around in his chair. He wanted to look at the people's faces.

"Sit still, Martin," his mother warned. "Listen to your daddy."

Martin took one last look around. "Maybe I'll be a preacher like Daddy," Martin said softly. "Then people will listen to me."

The Bus Boycott

Martin Luther King, Jr., did grow up and become a preacher. He became pastor of the Dexter Avenue Baptist Church in Montgomery, Alabama.

"Today is a sad day in Montgomery, Alabama," Reverend Martin Luther King, Jr., said. The people nodded.

"Today a woman named Rosa Parks was arrested.
She was arrested because she was Negro. She was
arrested because she was tired. She was too tired to give
up her seat on the bus to a white person."

"Yes, Reverend," the members of the church agreed.
They listened proudly to their new preacher.

15

"Well, now I am tired," Reverend King went on. "I am tired of riding buses that make Negroes sit in the back. I am tired of paying the same fare as white people, but being treated differently. I'm tired of the Jim Crow law. Until this law is changed, we should not ride on the buses."

"But how will we get to work?" someone asked.

"We'll help each other," Reverend King promised. "Those of us who can will walk."

"I am too old to walk that far," an older woman said sadly.

"I have a car, Sister. I'll pick you up every morning. Then I'll bring you home again in the evenings," a young man said.

"Your idea is wonderful, Reverend King," a young woman said. "We will tell our friends. They will not ride on the buses, either."

The Negro people of Alabama helped each other. People who had cars gave other people rides. Some walked miles to get to work and school. Many woke up before the sun rose to get to work on time. After a year, some people grew tired.

"The Jim Crow laws will never change," they said.

"Change takes time," Reverend King said quietly. "We must have faith. One day the laws will be changed."

In November of 1956, the law did change.

"Today is a great day in Montgomery, Alabama," the Reverend King said. "From this day on, we can ride on the buses. We can sit wherever we want."

The people cheered. They were grateful to
Reverend Martin Luther King, Jr.

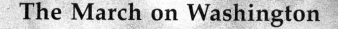

The March on Washington

Reverend King moved to Atlanta, Georgia. He worked with his father at the Ebenezer Baptist Church.

It was a hot summer day. Members of the church were having a picnic. Children played under the green trees. At a picnic table, some members were talking. They were not happy.

"You're right, Sister," a young man said. "One law was changed. If it wasn't for Reverend King, we would still be riding in the back of the buses. But other laws in the South are not fair. So much more needs to be done."

Martin Luther King, Jr., sat down at the table. "I've been thinking about those laws, Brothers and Sisters. They should be changed. In the North, you don't see 'Whites Only' signs. Everyone can use the water fountains. People can go to any restaurant. It should be that way in the South, too," Reverend King said. His voice was strong and quiet.

"But how can we get the laws changed?" one of the women asked.

"We can tell people how we feel. We can go to the place where the laws are made," Reverend King said.

"Washington!" a little boy said proudly.

Reverend King smiled down at him. "Right," he said. "We can march on Washington. We can tell people the laws are wrong."

"I'd like to go to Washington," the little boy said.

"We need to spread the word," Martin Luther King, Jr., said. "We need to let people know why we're going to Washington. We want our rights.

"People may want to stop us. They may push us. They may try to hold us back. But even if they hurt us, we will not hurt them. We will be peaceful."

The news of the March on Washington spread
quickly. Many people wanted to go with Reverend King.
They wanted the laws to change, too.

Buses left for Washington from all over the country.

Martin Luther King, Jr., and his group began their
trip. The bus stopped in a town along the way.

"Just where do you folks think you're going?" a man asked angrily.

"We're going to Washington. We're marching for our rights," someone answered.

"What rights?" the man asked. "Colored folks don't have any rights."

"We have the same rights as every American. Those are our civil rights," Reverend King said.

The man laughed again. "You are going to be marching for a long time," he said.

Martin became sad. He knew there were many
people like this man. They didn't think blacks should have
equal rights. The Reverend King and his followers would
have to make them see that they were wrong.

I Have a Dream

The August day was hot. Reverend Martin Luther King, Jr., walked onto the stage. People began to cheer and wave banners.

Reverend King spoke. "I have a dream that my four little children will one day...not be judged by the color of their skin but by the content of their character."

29

A hush fell over the crowd. Martin Luther King, Jr.,
looked out at the people. There were black people and
white people. There were young people and old people.
There were over two hundred thousand people in all.

"I have a dream that one day…little black boys and
black girls will be able to join hands with little white boys
and white girls and walk together as brothers and
sisters."

The people began to cheer again. But Reverend King went on.

"And if America is to be a great nation, this must become true. So let freedom ring!"

The crowd joined hands and looked up at Martin Luther King, Jr. They knew a great man was speaking. He was a man who would use peaceful ways to change the laws.

Martin Luther King, Jr., was a man who had a dream. But he said that he might not live to see his dream come true. He was right. In 1968, Martin Luther King, Jr., was shot and killed in Memphis, Tennessee.